A collection of Flags of the American Revolution, and those of the United States of America,

The Taunton Flag. 1774

Continental Navy Jack. 1775

The Gadsden Flag. 1775

Washington's Cruisers. 1775

The Bunker Hill Flag. 1775

Fort Moultrie Flag. 1776

Rhode Island. 1776

North Carolina Militia.

The Grand Union Flag. January 1, 1776

The Bennington Flag. 1777

The Stars and Stripes. June 14, 1777

The Alliances Flag. 1779

The Serapis Flag. 1779

United States Pennant. 1784

Star-Spangled Banner. 1794-1818 · 15 stars, 15 stripes.

Tennessee 1796. Ohio 1803. Louisiana 1812. Indiana 1816. Mississippi 1817. 1818-1819. 20 stars.

Illinois 1818. 1819-1820. 21 stars.

Alabama 1819. Maine 1800. 1820-1822. 23 stars.

Missouri 1821. 1822-1836. 24 stars.

Arkansas 1836. 1836-1837. 25 stars.

Michigan 1837. 1837-1845. 26 stars.

Fort McHenry near Baltimore, Md., as in 1814.

1. The Star-Spangled Banner.
2. Commanding Officer's Qtrs.
3. Soldiers' Barracks.
4. Powder Magazine.
5. Officers' Quarters.
6. The Dry Moat.
7. Sally Port.
8. Ravelin.
9. The Upper Battery.
10. The Lower Battery.
11. The Parade Ground.
12. Bastion.

Florida 1845. 1845-1846. 27 stars.

those of its Government and its Armed Force

Faithfully executed by Peter E. Spier. Anno 1973

Texas 1845.
1846=1847. 28 stars.

Iowa 1846.
1847=1848. 29 stars.

Wisconsin 1848.
1848=1851. 30 stars.

California 1850.
1851=1858. 31 stars.

Minnesota 1858.
1858=1859. 32 stars.

Oregon 1859.
1859=1861. 33 stars.

Kansas 1861.
1861=1863. 34 stars.

West Virginia 1863.
1863=1865. 35 stars.

Nevada 1864.
1865=1867. 36 stars.

Nebraska 1867.
1867=1877. 37 stars.

Colorado 1876.
1877=1890. 38 stars.

North Dakota, South Dakota,
Montana,
Washington 1889. Idaho 1890.
1890=1891. 43 stars.

Wyoming 1890.
1891=1896. 44 stars.

Utah 1896,
1896=1908. 45 stars.

Oklahoma 1907.
1908=1912. 46 stars.

New Mexico, Arizona 1912.
1912=1959. 48 stars.

Alaska 1959. Hawaii 1959.
1960. 50 stars.

The
President of
the United States.

Vice President of
the United States

Secretary of
Defense.

U.S. Army.

U.S. Navy.

U.S. Air Force

Secretary of
State.

Secretary of
Agriculture.

Other books by Peter Spier:

THE FOX WENT OUT ON A CHILLY NIGHT
LONDON BRIDGE IS FALLING DOWN
TO MARKET! TO MARKET!
THE ERIE CANAL
GOBBLE, GROWL, GRUNT
CRASH! BANG! BOOM!
FAST-SLOW, HIGH-LOW
THE STAR-SPANGLED BANNER
TIN-LIZZIE
NOAH'S ARK
OH, WERE THEY EVER HAPPY!
BORED—NOTHING TO DO!
THE LEGEND OF NEW AMSTERDAM
PEOPLE
PETER SPIER'S RAIN
PETER SPIER'S CHRISTMAS
THE BOOK OF JONAH
DREAMS
WE THE PEOPLE
PETER SPIER'S ADVENT CALENDAR:
    SILENT NIGHT, HOLY NIGHT
PETER SPIER'S BIRTHDAY CAKE

THE STAR-SPANGLED BANNER

This book is dedicated to the memory of
David S. Pallister Jr.
Captain, U.S.A.F.
22 June 1944 – 4 June 1969

Published by Doubleday, a division of Bantam Doubleday Dell Publishing Group, Inc.,
666 Fifth Avenue, New York, New York 10103. **Doubleday** and the portrayal of an anchor with a
dolphin are trademarks of Doubleday, a division of Bantam Doubleday Dell Publishing Group, Inc.

THE STAR-SPANGLED BANNER

Illustrated by Peter Spier

Doubleday

Library of Congress Catalog Card Number 73-79712. Illustrations Copyright © 1973 by Peter Spier.
All Rights Reserved. Printed in the United States of America:
ISBN: 0-385-09458-2 TRADE 0-385-07746-7 PREBOUND 0-385-23401-5 PAPERBACK

9 8 7 6 5

15   14   13   12   11

LBM

Oh, say can you see by the dawn's early light

What so proudly we hail'd at the twilight's last gleaming,

Whose broad stripes and bright stars

through the perilous fight

O'er the ramparts we watch'd were so gallantly streaming?

And the rockets' red glare, the bombs bursting in air,

Gave proof through the night that our flag was still there.

Oh, say does that star-spangled banner yet wave

O'er the land of the free and the home of the brave?

On the shore dimly seen through the mists of the deep,

Where the foe's haughty host in dread silence reposes,

What is that which the breeze, o'er the towering steep,

As it fitfully blows, half conceals, half discloses?

Now it catches the gleam of the morning's first beam,

In full glory reflected now shines in the stream.

'Tis the star-spangled banner, oh, long may it wave

O'er the land of the free and the home of the brave!

Oh, thus be it ever when freemen shall stand

Between their lov'd home and the war's desolation!

Blest with vict'ry and peace

may the heav'n-rescued land

Praise the power that hath made

and preserv'd us a nation!

Then conquer we must,

when our cause it is just,

And this be our motto, "In God is our Trust,"

And the star-spangled banner in triumph shall wave

O'er the land of the free and the home of the brave.

O say can you see ~~through~~ by the dawn's early light,
What so proudly we hail'd at the twilight's last gleaming,
Whose broad stripes & bright stars through the perilous fight
O'er the ramparts we watch'd, were so gallantly streaming?
And the rocket's red glare, the bomb bursting in air,
Gave proof through the night that our flag was still there,
O say does that star-spangled banner yet wave
O'er the land of the free & the home of the brave?

On the shore dimly seen through the mists of the deep,
Where the foe's haughty host in dread silence reposes,
What is that which the breeze, o'er the towering steep,
As it fitfully blows, half conceals, half discloses?
Now it catches the gleam of the morning's first beam,
In full glory reflected now shines in the stream,
'Tis the star-spangled banner — O long may it wave
O'er the land of the free & the home of the brave!

And where is that band who so vauntingly swore,
That the havoc of war & the battle's confusion
A home & a Country should leave us no more?
~~Their blood has~~
Their blood has wash'd out their foul footstep's pollution.
No refuge could save the hireling & slave
From the terror of flight or the gloom of the grave,
And the star-spangled banner in triumph doth wave
O'er the land of the free & the home of the brave.

O thus be it ever when freemen shall stand
Between their lov'd home & the war's desolation!
Blest with vict'ry & peace may the heav'n rescued land
Praise the power that hath made & preserv'd us a nation!
Then conquer we must, when our cause it is just,
And this be our motto — "In God is our trust,"
And the star-spangled banner in triumph shall wave
O'er the land of the free & the home of the brave. —

This is the poem Francis Scott Key wrote—it had no title then—in his Baltimore hotel room during the night of September 14, 1814, after witnessing the bombardment of Fort McHenry, and gave to his brother-in-law, J. H. Nicholson, the next day. This copy remained in the Nicholson family for almost a century, but the Maryland Historical Society bought it in 1953 for $26,400. Key made three more copies of the poem; one is owned by the Pennsylvania Historical Society, another by the Library of Congress. The third one has disappeared.

The United States was thirty-eight years old, George Washington had been dead for fifteen years, Benjamin Franklin almost twenty-five. Thomas Jefferson, author of the Declaration of Independence and third President, now seventy-two, would live another twelve years. A poverty-stricken family in the backwoods of Kentucky, the Lincolns, had, among their several children, a five-year-old named Abraham. The prosperous Lees of Virginia had a fourteen-year-old son, Robert E., and the United States of America had been at war with Great Britain for over two years in what would come to be known as the War of 1812. Ever since 1803, the year in which the Napoleanic wars began, England had been fighting for her very life against France and her allies. Due to the enormous demands of the Royal Navy, hundreds of seamen were serving the fleet; as a result, the number of British commercial ships or merchantmen was greatly diminished. American shippers quickly filled this void and made the trade between the French and Spanish colonies in the West Indies and Europe virtually their monopoly. The British, blockading France and French-occupied Europe, forbade this trade — even by neutrals — unless these ships first touched at an English port and submitted to inspection. Napoleon's "continental system," on the other hand, forbade the importation of any cargo into its territory that had been cleared by the British. The Americans, caught in between, evaded both rules and confiscation by putting into an American port before proceeding to Europe. By the Embargo Act of 1807, President Jefferson closed all American ports, halting trade, hoping thereby to force Britain and France to lift their restrictions on American shipping. This, however, turned out to be disastrous: tobacco, wheat and lumber piled up in warehouses and the hoped-for results were not achieved. The Royal Navy, in need of ever more men, began boarding American ships in order to return British deserters to the fleet, often taking Americans as well. Secretary of State James Madison in 1804 reported to Congress that 2,273 American seamen had been seized by the British in the past year. It should be added, however, that twenty-thousand British sailors were believed to be serving on American ships at the time, where wages and working conditions were better. From then on, American tempers, already on edge, flared over the troop seizure and other random incidents. On June 18, 1812, the United States declared war on Great Britain, a war for which the young nation was unprepared. In August, the British took Detroit, and an American attack on the British position at Niagara failed. At sea, things went better for the Americans: the U.S.S. *Constitution* was victorious against H.M.S. *Guerriere* and the U.S.S. *United States* captured H.M.S. *Macedonia*. But this period of victory did not last, and 1813 saw the Royal Navy capture scores of American ships while those that escaped were bottled up in port, and the Atlantic coast was blockaded. Many New England merchants, depending totally on world trade and opposed to the war from the start, now became openly hostile to the American participation in the conflict. But the war continued, with small actions and skirmishes. The British conducted landings and lightning raids, each time withdrawing to the safety of their ships. Meanwhile, things had gone well for the British in Europe: the French were finally defeated at Leipzig, Paris surrendered in March of 1814, and Napoleon abdicated in April. England was now free to concentrate her efforts on that bothersome distant war in the New World. On August 19th, a mighty British fleet entered Chesapeake Bay, landed a professional army,

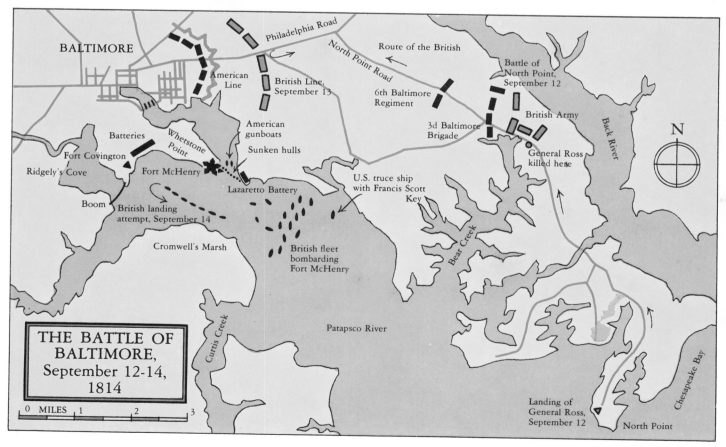

BALTIMORE

Philadelphia Road

North Point Road

Route of the British

Battle of North Point, September 12

American Line

British Line, September 13

6th Baltimore Regiment

British Army

Back River

3d Baltimore Brigade

N

Batteries

Whetstone Point

American gunboats

Sunken hulls

General Ross killed here

Fort Covington

Ridgely's Cove

Fort McHenry

Lazaretto Battery

U.S. truce ship with Francis Scott Key

Boom

British landing attempt, September 14

Bear Creek

Cromwell's Marsh

British fleet bombarding Fort McHenry

Curtis Creek

Patapsco River

Chesapeake Bay

THE BATTLE OF BALTIMORE, September 12-14, 1814

0 MILES 1   2   3

Landing of General Ross, September 12

North Point

Mr James Calhoun Jun Deputy Commissary

To Mary Pickersgill Dr

To 1 American Ensign 30 by 42½ feet first quality Bunting $405.90

To 1 — Do   Do   17 by 25½ feet ——— Do   pr   168.54

August 19th 1813   for Fort McHenry $5,74,44

Baltimore 27th October 1813 Recd from James Calhoun Jun
Deputy Commissary Two Hundred and twenty four Dollars
and forty four Cents in full for the above bill
                    signed duplicates
                              for Mary Pickersgill
                              Eliza Young

The original receipt for payment of the "Star-Spangled Banner," reproduced here with the kind permission of the Trustees of the Star-Spangled Banner Flag House in Baltimore, shows that Mary Young Pickersgill was paid for sewing ". . . 1 American Ensign 30 by 42 feet first quality Bunting $405.90," and $168.54 for a smaller flag. The original Star-Spangled Banner, rather the worse for wear, is now prominently displayed in the Smithsonian Institution in Washington, D.C. The Flag House, once the home of Mary Pickersgill, also preserves several pieces of it. It is curious to note that the National Park Service, which administers Fort McHenry National Monument, purchased a nylon replica of the original flag for $637 in 1971.

which promptly defeated the raw American militia at Bladensburg, captured Washington, D.C. (then a small town of six thousand), and burned the Capitol Building, the President's house and other government buildings. On August 25, afraid of being cut off from their supplies, the British left the city and returned to their ships. It was to Baltimore, with forty-thousand inhabitants and the country's third largest city, that the British now turned their attention. This had been expected by the American troops and the city's defenses had been greatly strengthened. Fort McHenry, guarding the sea approaches, had been strengthened and old ships' hulls placed in position to be sunk at a moment's notice, to block the main channel to the city. On Sunday, September 11, the British fleet arrived at the mouth of the Patapsco River, and Baltimore's church bells called the militia to arms. The next day the British landed at North Point and began moving toward the city. In one of the first encounters with the

1814 Congreve rocket of 32 lbs.
1: wooden stabilizing shaft, 15' long.   2: fuse. 3: warhead.
4: iron body containing propelling charge.

13" bomb of 190 lbs. 1: fuse. 2: powder charge.

Americans, the British General Ross was killed. After a short battle the militia retreated toward the city into prepared positions. It had been the British plan to take the city both from land and sea, but Fort McHenry stood solidly in the way of the ships. It was manned by a varied assortment of one-thousand troops and commanded by Major George Armistead, U.S.A. The twenty-four ships' hulks had been sunk, booms placed across the north branch of the Patapsco River, and all the outlying fortifications were manned. Since the river was too shallow for the larger British ships, sixteen smaller vessels (including five bomb ships and one rocket ship) moved into position two miles from the fort, and at the dawn of September 13, commenced their bombardment. The fort's thirty-two-pounders joined the fight but ceased firing when they found that the range was too great. The heavy shelling and rocketing, with a new rocket recently invented by William Congreve, continued. At one A.M., on September 14, the British attempted to land a force of 1,000 men at Ferry Branch in order to attack the fort from the rear, but they were discovered and retreated downriver, shot at by every American gun that would bear. The bombardment lasted for twenty-five hours, with a few intermissions, and at nine in the morning of the fourteenth, the British withdrew. The assault had failed. Between 1,500 and 1,800 shells—some weighing two hundred twenty pounds—had been fired at the fort, and it seems a miracle that the defenders lost only four men killed and twenty-four wounded. On land the British did not fare much better. Facing the firmly entrenched Americans on the city's outskirts, the British decided that taking the city without naval support would prove too costly and so they retreated toward North Point. They re-embarked the next day and sailed toward the open Atlantic.

In the meantime, American and British peace-making delegates were meeting in Ghent (in today's Belgium), and they signed a peace treaty on December 24, 1814. But news traveled slowly in those days, and the last battle of the war was fought more than two weeks after the peace had been signed, when Andrew Jackson defeated the British at New Orleans on January 8, 1815.

The war had accomplished absolutely nothing for either side, and the very reasons for which the United States had gone to war—the inspection of American vessels and the impressment of their sailors—were not even mentioned in the treaty. But more than a century later the United States did get something totally unexpected out of the war: a national anthem! This is how it came about.

During their withdrawal from Washington, D.C., the British had arrested Dr. William Beanes, a physician from Upper Marlboro, for ordering the imprisonment of three of their stragglers, and they planned to take him to Halifax, Nova Scotia, for trial. Francis Scott Key, a friend of Beanes, practiced law in Georgetown. Armed with a letter from President Madison, he rode on horseback to Baltimore on September 4th to try to obtain the release of Dr. Beanes. The next day he and John S. Skinner, a U.S. agent in charge of prisoner exchange, left Baltimore on a small vessel, flying the flag of truce, to find the British fleet cruising nearby at the mouth of the Potomac. Two days later they went aboard H.M.S. *Tonnant*, the British Admiral Cochrane's flagship. The admiral listened patiently, but firmly refused Key's request on the grounds that Dr. Beanes, a civilian, not only had interfered in military matters, but had also broken a pledge binding him to neutrality. Key, an experienced lawyer, argued that Dr. Beanes at his advanced age might not have realized what he was doing, and that he, moreover, had given British wounded men excellent medical care, showing the admiral letters from British prisoners that proved his point. Cochrane relented but ordered Key, Skinner and Beanes not to return to Baltimore since they had heard and seen too much of the British preparations against the city. They were returned to their own vessel, and from there they watched the beginning of the bombardment of Fort McHenry when dawn broke on September 13. When dusk fell the American flag still flew over the ramparts. During the night—the time of the landing attempt at Ferry Branch—the shelling stopped abruptly. After a short, eerie silence a deafening cannonade broke out: It was the Americans repulsing the landing force. Key did not know this and assumed it to be the final assault on the fort; then the

bombardment resumed in full force and at dawn he saw a flag hanging limply from its pole over the fort, but he was unable to tell whether it was British or American. Then the breeze slowly unfolded the stars and stripes! Key had been writing poetry for years, and, greatly moved, jotted down a stanza on the back of a letter he carried in his pocket. When the British withdrew, the Americans sailed for Baltimore and Key continued work on his poem. That night in his lodgings at the Indian Queen Hotel he finished the first draft of the poem. The next morning he showed it to Judge Nicholson, his brother-in-law, who liked it so much that he had it printed immediately as "The Defense of Fort McHenry" and, it is told, suggested that a well-known old tune called "To Anacreon in Heaven" would go well with it. On September 20th, several local papers printed the poem, too, and in October the program of a Baltimore theater announced that "After the Play, Mr. Harding will sing a much admired SONG, written by a gentleman of Maryland, in commemoration of the GALLANT DEFENSE OF FORT McHENRY, called THE STAR-SPANGLED BANNER." Over the years, it gained so much in popularity that, in 1904, the Navy was ordered to play it at all ceremonial occasions, and in 1916, President Wilson proclaimed it the national anthem for all the armed forces. But it was not until 1931 that it officially became the nation's national anthem. Within the United States, the American flag is permitted to be flown twenty-four hours a day in only eleven locations. Fort McHenry is one of them, the birthplace of Francis Scott Key is another. And a third place is his grave in Frederick, Maryland.

FRANCIS SCOTT KEY, 1779–1843. Portrait by D. Clinton Peters after an original attributed to Rembrandt Peale.

Words by
FRANCIS SCOTT KEY
(1779–1843)

Music by
J. STAFFORD SMITH
(1750–1836)

proof through the night that our flag was still there. Oh, say does that__ star-span-gled

ban-ner__ yet__ wave__ O'er the land__ of the free and the home of the brave?

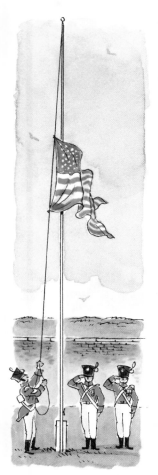

2. On the shore dimly seen through the mists of the deep,
Where the foe's haughty host in dread silence reposes,
What is that which the breeze,o'er the towering steep,
As it fitfully blows, half conceals, half discloses?
Now it catches the gleam of the morning's first beam,
In full glory reflected now shines in the stream.
'Tis the star-spangled banner, oh, long may it wave
O'er the land of the free and the home of the brave!

3. And where is that band who so vauntingly swore
That the havoc of war and the battle's confusion
A home and a country should leave us no more?
Their blood has wash'd out their foul footstep's pollution.
No refuge could save the hireling and slave
From the terror of flight or the gloom of the grave,
And the star-spangled banner in triumph doth wave
O'er the land of the free and the home of the brave.

4. Oh, thus be it ever when freemen shall stand
Between their lov'd home and the war's desolation!
Blest with vict'ry and peace may the heav'n-rescued land
Praise the power that hath made and preserv'd us a nation!
Then conquer we must, when our cause it is just,
And this be our motto, "In God is our Trust,"
And the star-spangled banner in triumph shall wave
O'er the land of the free and the home of the brave.

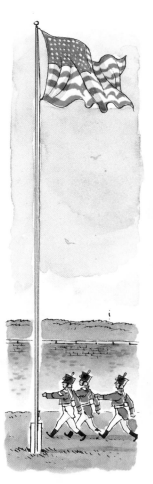

Secretary of Commerce.

Secretary of the Interior.

Attorney General.

Sec'y. of Labor.

Postmaster General.

Secretary of the Treasury.

Secretary of H. E. W.

Chief of Staff, U.S. Air Force.

General, U.S. Air Force.

Group Standard, U.S. Air Force.

Chief of Staff, U.S. Army.

General of the Army

General, U.S. Army

Major General, Medical Corps.

Major General, Chaplains Corps.

Headquarters, Army Ground Forces.

Marking Pennant, Commission Pennant.

Organizational Color, U.S.A.

Organizational Standard, U.S.A.

Adj. General Maryland National Guard.

Color, U.S. Corps of Cadets.

Survey Flag, Coast and Geodetic Survey.

Director, Coast and Geodetic Survey.

Consular Boat Flag, Foreign Service.

United States Customs Service.

U.S. Immigration Service.

Yacht Ensign.

Geological Survey.

Director, Fish and Wildlife Service.

Surgeon General, Public Health Service.

Fleet Admiral.

THE STANDARD PROPORTIONS OF THE UNITED STATES FLAG AND FLAG NOMENCLATURE.

1. Truck.
2. Staff.
3. Canton.
4. Field.
5. Hoist.
6. Fly.
7. Fly end.
8. Halyard.

Hoist of flag 1.; Fly of flag 1.9; Hoist of union .5385; Fly of union .76; A .054; B .054; C .063; D .063; Diameter of star .0616; Width of stripe .0769.

Admiral.

Senior Officer Present.

Church Pennant.

Vice Admiral.

Rear Admiral.

Commodore.

Broad Command Pennant.

Burgee Command Pennant.

Merchant Marine, U.S.N.R.

Commission Pennant.

Presidential Unit Citation.

Battle Efficiency Pennant.

Yacht Owners Pennant, Naval Reserve.

Union Jack.

U.S.M.C. Standard.

U.S.M.C Guidon.

Commandant, U.S.M.C.

Lt. General, U.S.M.C.

Maj. General, U.S.M.C.

Guidon, Organizational, U.S.M.C.

Admiral, U.S.C.G.

Ensign, U.S.C.G.

Vice Admiral, U.S.C.G.

Rear Admiral, U.S.C.G.

Pennant, U.S.C.G.

Senior Officer Present.

Commodore, U.S.C.G.

Guidon.

U.S. Coast Guard.

Broad Command Pennant, U.S.C.G.

Burgee Command Pennant.